The All-Token

How NFTs Will Change Our Purchase, Sales, and Production Processes

Koso Brown

Copyright 2024© Koso Brown

All rights reserved. This book is copyrighted and no part of it may be reproduced, distributed, or transmitted in any form or by any means, including photocopying, recording, or other electronic or mechanical methods, without the prior written permission of the publisher, except in the case of brief quotations embodied in critical reviews and certain other non-commercial uses permitted by copyright law.

Printed in the United States of America Copyright 2024© Koso Brown

Contents

- Introduction 1
- Chapter 1 2
- Definition and meaning of NFT 2
  - Why are NFTs important? 4
- Chapter 2 5
- How are NFTs purchased? 5
  - Get a cryptocurrency wallet open 5
- Chapter 3 8
- NFT benefits 8
  - What is a marketplace for NFTs? 9
- Chapter 4 13
- NFTs: How are they made? 13
  - How Will NFTs Affect Traditional Art Markets? 17
- Chapter 5 19
- NFT Obstacles in the Art Industry 19
  - NFT marketplace examples 21
- Chapter 6 23
- Creating an NFT 23
- Chapter 7 30
- Why Are NFTs Gaining Adoption? 30
  - Potential NFT Drawbacks 32
  - NFTs' Future and Its Effect on Society 33
- Conclusion 36

Introduction

Non-fungible tokens (NFTs) have countless applications. They are a key component of Web3 and the point where the digital and physical worlds converge. What benefits does this new technology provide? A financial journalist could recognize the opportunity to avert a financial catastrophe. The opportunity to create a community out of an audience for a marketer. The chance for a human rights advocate providing marginalized populations with an official identity. Still, we're assuming too much. Let's examine the development of this technology and the problems it aimed to address to comprehend the idea behind NFTs. Scarcity in the digital era is nonexistent. The notion that value and meaning are created by scarcity has its roots in human history and culture. The demand for limited resources has fueled advancement, ingenuity, and inventiveness. It is the primary force behind human evolution. A world devoid of shortages? The World Wide Web existed like that before blockchain. Our information, art, and music are shaped by an endless number of bits and bytes. quickly duplicated and dispersed.

Digital artists thus found it difficult to make money off of their creations. Nonetheless, some would contest the current quo.

Chapter 1

Definition and meaning of NFT

The acronym for "non-fungible token" is NFT. Something that is non-fungible is special and cannot be replicated. In contrast, cryptocurrencies and fiat money are interchangeable, meaning they may be bought, sold, or otherwise swapped for one another. Each NFT is distinct because it has a digital signature. Digital assets, or NFTs for short, might be images, movies, audio files, or other digital formats. Examples of NFTs include comic books, trading cards, games, sports souvenirs, artwork, and more.

Unlike stocks, bonds, and other conventional investments, nonfungible tokens (NFTs) are seen as an alternative investment that cannot be exchanged for another similar thing. NFTs and rare items are comparable. They became more and more in demand in 2020 and 2021. As a result of celebrities, content producers, auction houses, and other players entering the market, the cost of digital artwork increased.

What is the process by which NFTs operate?

The ownership of the NFT is established by blockchain technology. Blockchain functions as a decentralized ledger, making it possible for NFTs to have public authentication. The technique verifies the originality and ownership of the work using a digital signature. Instead of owning a work of art to display on a wall, an NFT buyer receives a digital copy of the artwork together with a digital certificate of authenticity.

The item's trademark and copyright are not owned by the NFT buyer. NFT purchasers have an original in the virtual world, notwithstanding the possibility that there are several variations available online. It is possible to build royalties into the token so that artists will eventually get paid a percentage of sales.

In general, NFTs are not divisible. The token, which is the fundamental unit of the NFT, is typically not convertible into lower denominations, unlike dimes, which may be split into ten. However, other platforms, like Fractional, have lately introduced the concept of fractional ownership of NFTs. An NFT can be split up into smaller NFTs and sold to different buyers thanks to fractional ownership.

NFTs are also unchangeable. Once blockchain technology has been used to encode them, they cannot be changed. The item's authenticity and uniqueness are confirmed by the blockchain that stores it.

Why are NFTs important?

According to Justin Herzig, co-founder of Own the Moment NFT, which offers content, tools, and analytics on NFTs, the reason for the rise in popularity of NFTs is their "improved ease of onboarding, speculative nature as both a collectible and investment and grassroots communities developed around the products."

NFTs open up new avenues for people to purchase and sell digital assets. They facilitate the digital exhibition of artistic abilities by artists and other content creators, and they offer a digital ledger for the safe valuation, purchase, and exchange of digital art. New and previously decentralized actors can create creative value exchanges to create new market structures by using NFTs.

According to Herzig, NFTs are a prominent type of alternative investment that appeals to investors' passions and individual interests. Retail investors will be able to invest through NFTs in both personally meaningful and financially and functionally valuable assets. Like any investment, the buyer of NFT believes that the token's value will rise over time. Similar to their fungible counterparts, supply and demand fluctuations can affect NFTs. Grand View Research estimates that the NFT market will reach $211.72 billion by 2030, from its 2022 valuation of $20.44 billion.

Chapter 2

How are NFTs purchased?

Chap Because of its high level of risk and its abrupt highs and lows, even seasoned investors may be put off by the NFT market. If you're considering purchasing NFTs, you must comprehend the procedure. Let's examine the procedures involved:

Create an account on a cryptocurrency exchange

Making an account on a cryptocurrency platform or exchange is the first step. An online marketplace where various cryptocurrency kinds can be bought and sold is called a crypto exchange. You must register for an account on your preferred platform to purchase NFTs. It's important to investigate various platforms to determine which one best meets your needs in terms of features, costs, and continuing support.

Get a cryptocurrency wallet open.

The keys that allow you to access your digital assets are kept in a cryptocurrency wallet. To access their wallet, users are given a special seed phrase, also known as a recovery phrase.

You can't access your wallet without your seed phrase, therefore it's critical to keep it secure.

Wallets have two options: they can run independently or be hosted on an exchange. You still own responsibility for your wallet and private keys if they function on their own. If an exchange hosts your digital wallet, the exchange serves as a middleman for the transmission of cryptocurrency. The business is in charge of safeguarding your assets and has your private keys.

On the other hand, you need a wallet that is connected to the blockchain directly if you wish to buy and sell NFTs without the assistance of a third party. This enables the public key to be used for direct money transfers between individuals.

Wallets come in two varieties, referred to as "hot" or "cold":

Hot wallets are:

- ✓ Cyberattacks are more likely to occur than with cold wallets
- ✓ Web-based wallets, software
- ✓ Accessible as an in-browser extension, a desktop or mobile application, or both

Cold wallets are:

- ✓ But you run a higher danger of losing it, and you won't have a backup if you misplace your seed phrase.

- ✓ Hardware wallets are tangible, internet-unconnected gadgets
- ✓ Regarded as safer

Since the Ethereum blockchain is the network on which the majority of NFTs are sold, the cryptocurrency wallet you choose should preferably be able to interact with Ether (ETH, Ethereum), which is native to the Ethereum blockchain.

Transfer Ethereum into a crypto wallet

After choosing an NFT exchange and purchasing ETH, you must move the money to a wallet. Depending on the wallet you use, the exchange you use to purchase ETH and the marketplace where you want to trade NFTs, this procedure will alter.

Purchase NFTs

Upon connecting and funding your wallet, you can begin purchasing NFTs. An NFT becomes your property when you purchase it, therefore you effectively become the owner. Other rights to the work, such as the ability to reproduce or modify it, are not granted to the NFT holder unless they are specifically mentioned in the written contract between the buyer and the author. The NFT you bought can be subject to various restrictions from different marketplaces.

Chapter 3

NFT benefits

NFTs provide several benefits for collectors, other creators, and digital artists. Among the most significant advantages are the following:

- ❖ **Improved usefulness and interaction:** NFTs can include interactive components in addition to static digital files, providing collectors with a distinctive and engaging experience. Certain NFTs, for instance, provide access to special occasions, first-rate experiences, digital goods, or content associated with the artwork or collectible. This may increase the fidelity of customers.

- ❖ **Accessible investing and fractional ownership:** NFTs facilitate fractional ownership, allowing several people to jointly own a digital asset. Individual collectors who might not otherwise be able to buy one can participate and invest in high-value objects thanks to fractional ownership. In the NFT realm, this democratization of ownership opens up new opportunities for collectors and artists alike.

- ❖ **Royalties:** Through NFTs, artists can incorporate

royalties into their creations, guaranteeing a portion of future sales when the piece is resold on secondary markets. Even after the first sale, this feature allows artists to profit from the rising value of their works. Furthermore, royalties encourage collectors to help artists and further the development of the NFT ecosystem as a whole.

❖ **Unchangeable authenticity and ownership.** With NFTs, owners can validate the legitimacy and unchangeable ownership of a digital item. Its provenance, ownership, and transaction history are confirmed via distinctive NFT metadata. This guarantees that the ownership of an NFT can be quickly and simply confirmed using blockchain technology, giving owners peace of mind and trust.

❖ **Direct monetization:** NFTs allow digital artists to make money off of their creations directly from online markets like Niio, eliminating the need for galleries, auction houses, or other middlemen.

What is a marketplace for NFTs?

Although the NFT market is always changing, the majority of NFT marketplaces usually fit into one of these three categories:

- ❖ **A proprietary marketplace:** is one where the business running it offers NFTs that are protected by trademarks or copyrights.

- ❖ **Closed marketplace:** To participate, artists must submit an application, and the marketplace typically handles the minting procedures. More limitations apply to trading and selling.
- ❖ **Open market:** NFTs can be bought, sold, or minted by anybody. The process of releasing your token on the blockchain in a unique way so that it may be purchased is known as minting. Although creators can also mint their works, open marketplaces usually mint NFTs for you.

To be informed when there are new NFT drops, some NFT traders register and subscribe to accounts on many marketplaces. Along with more specialist investing platforms like Rarity Sniper and Rarity Tools, information about new NFTs is also exchanged on Discord and Twitter. Upon the announcement of highly anticipated NFTs, investors typically move swiftly.

The majority of marketplaces provide consumers with step-by-step instructions to help them learn how to use them. After making an account on the marketplace, you ought to link your wallet to it. Certain marketplaces employ their proprietary wallet, or you can create one right from within the website. Discounts or a decrease in the extra costs associated with utilizing external wallets may be available when using a marketplace's private wallet.

What applications and instances do NFTs have?

A 2017 game called Crypto Kitties, in which players could buy and sell virtual kittens, was one of the first applications of NFTs. NFTs that garnered attention in 2021 were Jack Dorsey, the CEO of Twitter, and work by Beeple, the alias of artist Mike Winkelmann, whose artwork "Everyday: The First 5000 Days" brought in $69 million.

A variety of virtual assets and collectibles are being sold using NFTs, such as the following:

- ✓ Real-world assets that have been tokenized, like property.
- ✓ Decentraland is a 3D virtual reality (VR) platform that offers virtual real estate.
- ✓ Taco Bell commissioned a range of GIFs and photos,

with the proceeds going to the restaurant chain's charitable foundation.
- ✓ CryptoPunks are virtual collectible characters.
- ✓ The initial meme of Nyan Cat
- ✓ A complete studio album released by Kings of Leon.
- ✓ Trading cards with actor William Shatner's items.
- ✓ Digital trading cards for the National Basketball Association.
- ✓ Nike digital sneaker.

Today, amateurs with a keen interest in a domain or project make up the majority of NFT owners and collectors. But as products and technology advance, NFTs should eventually become commonplace and draw in retail investors.

Chapter 4

NFTs: How are they made?

Smart contracts are used to generate NFTs. When a token is generated or minted, a smart contract code is integrated. The smart contract, which is kept on the blockchain, establishes the attributes of the NFT, including ownership and transferability.

The terms and conditions of an agreement are contained directly inside the lines of code of the autonomous smart contract. A smart contract that operates on top of the distributed ledger and stores a single token is connected to each NFT, ensuring verifiable uniqueness and ownership. The unique token that verifies ownership of the NFT can only be owned by one individual, even though duplicates of the same content exist.

One essential component of blockchain technology is smart contracts. Although the Ethereum blockchain hosts a large number of NFTs, other blockchain technologies like Tron and Neo serve as the foundation for other NFTs. Blockchain further contributes to the security of NFTs.

Market players and watchers are becoming more conscious of NFTs' environmental impact as they become more popular. Greenhouse gases produced by blockchain use have a major impact on the global carbon footprint.

Examining NFTs' Potential to Transform the World

The following examples demonstrate how NFTs can greatly enhance and streamline some practical use cases.

The Creator Economy and Digital Assets

The way we think about digital assets and the creator economy is being completely transformed by NFTs. Digital trading cards, artwork, and other unique digital goods are NFTs that may be purchased, sold, and exchanged on the Ethereum network.

Creators can create these NFTs, which allow them to claim ownership and monetize their digital works. The ability to create NFT collections is another feature that gives digital object ownership and collection a whole new meaning. The blockchain's smart contracts make it possible to buy, sell, and trade these NFTs safely and transparently. NFTs are giving creators new ways to get money for their work and giving collectors a way to own and exchange exclusive digital goods.

Lending and Renting

NFTs have the potential to develop a platform for the loan and rental of tangible assets like real estate, luxury goods, and automobiles. This could improve who can access and use these resources and open up new sources of income for the owners.

Authenticity and Ownership Verification

An item's ownership and authenticity can be established by using NFTs to affix a distinct digital token to it. This is helpful in sectors where provenance matters, including the art and luxury goods industries.

Real-world Resources

Luxury automobiles, fine art, and real estate are examples of real-world assets that can be represented by NFTs. This improves transaction transparency and trust while also making it simpler for individuals to participate in these assets.

Gaming

One of the most interesting sectors where NFTs are having a significant influence is the gaming business. In video games, NFTs can be used to produce one-of-a-kind, customized in-game things like armor, weaponry, and other virtual commodities.

Gamers now have an additional means of making money off of their in-game accomplishments when they trade and sell these products on the open market. In addition, it eliminates the problem of "game-item fraud," makes gaming more interesting and immersive, and provides publishers and developers with new sources of income.

Chain of Supply

By giving each link in the supply chain a digital, tamper-proof record, NFTs can enhance supply chain management. It is feasible to trace the flow of commodities in real-time and make sure they are manufactured, handled, and transported ethically and sustainably by describing each step as an NFT. This can improve supply chain accountability and transparency, which will make it simpler to spot and resolve problems like environmental degradation and human rights abuses.

Identity Verification

NFTs can offer a safe and unchangeable method of identity verification, which is helpful for sectors including government, healthcare, and finance. An NFT that serves as a person's identity can be created to record details about that individual, including name, date of birth, and government-issued identification number, and to enable safe, tamper-proof identity verification.

Tickets for Airlines

NFTs could allow airline tickets to be genuinely owned, providing customers greater freedom and control over their trip arrangements. A distinct NFT would serve as the ticket's representation rather than a physical or digital one, enabling it to be purchased and traded on an open market like OpenSea. In the same way that tickets for concerts or sporting events are now bought and sold, this would establish a secondary market for airline tickets that is more effective and transparent.

How Will NFTs Affect Traditional Art Markets?

In short, the answer is that NFTs can upend established art markets. Here's the procedure:

Increased Openness

Traditional art marketplaces lack the transparency offered by NFTs. Since each NFT is validated on a blockchain, it is simple to determine who owns it and whether it is authentic. This makes it far more difficult for copies or forgeries, which are a prevalent problem in the traditional art market, to be sold as authentic works.

New Sources of Income

NFTs give collectors and artists new sources of income. For instance, an artist may offer an original piece of art for sale as an NFT and subsequently market prints or other products based on the piece.

Similar to how traditional art collectors can resell pieces in their collections, collectors can likewise profit from the sale of NFTs they have acquired.

Market Expansion

Because NFTs make art more accessible to a wider range of customers, they may also contribute to the market's expansion. High-end art is only affordable for a limited portion of the population in traditional art markets. Conversely, NFTs make digital art accessible to anyone with an internet connection, expanding the market to a far wider audience.

Enhanced Easily Accessible

The fact that NFTs facilitate the sale of artwork by artists and the acquisition of it by collectors is among its greatest advantages. With NFTs, artists may sell their creations to consumers directly, doing away with the need for middlemen like galleries or auction houses.

This implies that while purchasers will be able to purchase art at a reduced price, artists will receive a higher percentage of the revenues from their sales.

Chapter 5

NFT Obstacles in the Art Industry

NFTs can upend established art markets, but there are a few challenges that need to be addressed:

Environmental Apprehensions

The influence of blockchain networks on the environment is another problem that NFTs deal with. Concerns regarding the technology's carbon footprint are raised by the substantial energy required to create and verify NFTs.

For collectors and artists who care about sustainability and the effects their acts have on the environment, this is particularly difficult.

Physical Illness

Some collectors might be reluctant to invest in NFTs as they lack the tangible quality of traditional art. NFTs don't have the same financial worth as actual art, even though they offer provenance and authenticity.

For those collectors who enjoy the tactile aspect of owning and putting on display actual art, this could make the pieces less enticing.

There Is No Regulation

One of the biggest issues NFTs in the art industry are facing is the absence of regulation. Although there is some transparency offered by blockchain networks, there are currently no laws protecting buyers or sellers from fraud or other problems.

Is NFT Art Art?

The medium of art has been used for centuries and doesn't seem to be slowing down. It's a means for people to employ color, texture, and shape to reflect on life and represent who they are. As a result, it appears that only those who want to define the parameters of art are interested in the discussion over whether NFTs qualify as art.

But the art market is another matter entirely. Although it generates billions of dollars in revenue annually, this industry has been sluggish to adjust to emerging technologies and shifts in consumer preferences.

This is beginning to change, as an increasing number of collectors are using non-fungible tokens (NFTs) in the hopes of locating exceptional, one-of-a-kind artwork at costs within their means.

The problem is that, despite the claims of some, NFTs are not the ideal medium for creating art because they rely on an ecosystem that doesn't seem to be designed with art in mind.

NFTs are intended to be bought, sold, traded, and swapped. They are a system based on commodities and the concepts of rarity and scarcity. The model employed by conventional art markets, which emphasizes subjective value over objective value, is substantially different from this one.

It's important to remember that art is also continuously developing, pushing boundaries, and breaking down barriers; as such, it cannot be constrained by institutions or centralized methods.

Furthermore, although Web3 ecosystems and NFTs are still in their infancy, they provide artists with lots of chances to experiment and push the boundaries of their medium.

NFT marketplace examples

Numerous NFT marketplaces are available. Some instances are:

Rarible

A platform built on Ethereum that makes it easier to create, sell, and acquire ownership rights to digital art through NFTs.

Nifty Gateway

Collections by well-known artists working in fine art, animation, video, and mixed media are available at Nifty Gateway. Buyers looking to trade or collect art with long-term worth are the target audience for this website.

NBA Top Shot

Basketball aficionados can swap basketball video clips on this NFT marketplace. NBA Top Shot boasts a sizable fan base and challenges and competitions provide a social element.

OpenSea

OpenSea, one of the biggest NFT marketplaces, provides NFTs in a variety of categories, including collectibles, sports, games, music, fashion, and art. Users can also access a variety of educational resources on the website.

Chapter 6

Creating an NFT

Making an NFT only takes a few basic steps to complete. The first step in creating an NFT is for the creator to digitally represent their asset—which could be a song, artwork, or collectible. After that, the digital asset needs to be uploaded to a blockchain so that it may be stored and confirmed there.

Usually, a smart contract—a self-executing contract kept on the blockchain—is used for this. The NFT's ownership transfer guidelines are contained in the smart contract, which also makes sure that the asset can only be transferred by these guidelines.

Launching the NFT

The NFT is given to the asset creator after it has been uploaded to the blockchain. This implies that the person who created the NFT now owns the asset and is free to sell or otherwise dispose of it.

The NFT is simple to trace and verify because it is kept on the blockchain and its ownership is noted in a public ledger.

Transferring an NFT's Ownership

The ownership of the NFT is passed from the seller to the buyer after the buyer has transferred the coin. A smart contract is used for this, which automatically updates the public ledger to reflect the ownership change.

The NFT can now be exchanged, sold, or kept as a collectible after being placed in the buyer's wallet.

Keeping and overseeing NFTs

Because NFTs are kept on the blockchain, managing and accessing them is simple. They can be kept in a secure, encrypted digital wallet like MetaMask or MyEtherWallet, which lets users manage their NFTs and cryptocurrency.

Users can see, trade, and manage their assets with these wallets, which also provide them with access to their NFTs.

Blockchain Technology and NFTs

A recent development in blockchain technology is the creation, ownership, and exchange of distinct digital assets through Non-Fungible Tokens (NFTs). This creative application of blockchain technology is completely changing our understanding of digital content ownership and value.

- ✓ Since a transaction entered into the blockchain is an immutable ledger, it cannot be changed or removed. Because ownership records cannot be altered or manipulated, NFTs provide a safe means of storing and exchanging digital assets.
- ✓ One of the primary characteristics of NFTs is their decentralized network architecture, which means that ownership is tracked on the blockchain rather than being governed by a single entity.
- ✓ It is simple to confirm who is the owner of an NFT at any given time because NFT ownership is documented on the blockchain. This enables the tracking of an NFT's ownership history, which is crucial in the art industry and other fields that place a premium on provenance and authenticity.

NFTs in the Field of Art

The art world is greatly impacted by Non-Fungible Tokens (NFTs), which give artists a fresh and creative outlet for the sale and distribution of their creations. Artists now have more options to reach new audiences and make money because of the special qualities of NFTs, like verifiable ownership and the creation of unique digital assets.

- ❖ **Intellectual Property Protection:** NFTs give artists a transparent, safe method to safeguard their creations. In the event of a dispute or infringement, artists will find it simpler to establish their ownership of a work thanks to the blockchain's permanent record of ownership and transfers.
- ❖ **Enhanced Visibility:** Through NFTs, artists can expand their audience and draw attention to their work. Artists can reach new audiences who might not have been able to buy their work through regular means by offering it as NFTs.
- ❖ **New Revenue Streams:** Outside of the traditional art market, NFTs enable artists to sell their creations as distinct digital assets. An artist might, for instance, offer a limited edition of their piece as an NFT, giving collectors a new opportunity to acquire it and

enabling artists to make extra money.

- ❖ **Direct Sales to Collectors:** Through NFTs, artists, and collectors can transact directly, enabling artists to charge collectors for their creations without the need for middlemen. This can boost the income of artists and give collectors a simpler, more affordable option to buy digital artworks.
- ❖ **Authenticity and provenance:** NFTs offer a clear, safe means of confirming the rightful owner and authenticity of digital artworks. This is particularly significant in the art industry, where a work's authenticity and provenance play a major role in establishing its value. Artists can use NFTs to make sure that the ownership history of their work can be easily verified and that the piece is legitimate.

NFTs in Virtual Reality and Gaming

The use of Non-Fungible Tokens (NFTs) in virtual reality and gaming is evolving. With NFTs, gamers and VR users may now own exclusive digital assets and engage with the virtual world in fresh and creative ways.

- ❖ **Increased Immersion:** NFTs give consumers a fresh perspective on virtual reality and gaming. Users can feel more connected to and in control of the virtual environment when they own exclusive digital assets, which heightens immersion and fosters new kinds of interaction.

- ❖ **New Play Forms:** NFTs allow users an additional way to engage and play in the virtual environment. Users can, for instance, possess exclusive digital goods that let them progress in games or engage with the virtual environment in novel ways. As a result, there is an increase in interaction and engagement with the virtual environment.

NFTs in Entertainment and Music

Non-Fungible Tokens (NFTs) are transforming the music and entertainment sectors by giving performers, musicians, and artists a new avenue for revenue generation and audience interaction.

- ❖ **Direct Distribution:** NFTs give performers, musicians, and artists a way to connect directly with their audience. This gives artists more control over their work and direct access to fans by doing away with the need for middlemen like record companies or music streaming services.

- ❖ **Monetizing Creative Work:** New Forms of Revenue (NFTs) are a novel means of generating income for performers, musicians, and artists. Selling distinctive digital assets, such as original songs, films, and other kinds of creative content, is part of this. NFTs give creative professionals access to a new source of income by ensuring that the ownership of these assets can be readily verified.
- ❖ **Fan Interaction:** NFTs give performers, musicians, and artists a fresh avenue to interact with their audience. This can involve giving fans a new avenue to interact with their favorite performers and artists by offering limited-edition goods or unique experiences through NFTs.

Chapter 7

Why Are NFTs Gaining Adoption?

Originality in Art
Another reason NFTs are growing in popularity is that they provide creatives and artists more freedom. Creatives and artists can sell their products directly to consumers using NFTs, eliminating the need for a middleman. They can now set their prices and have more influence over the work they do.

Absence of a Middleman
Because NFTs do away with the need for middlemen, they are growing in popularity. NFTs allow people to buy and sell digital assets directly to one another, without the need of a middleman. Transactions are therefore more affordable, quicker, and secure.

Potential for Investment
Because NFTs have the potential to be investments, they are also growing in popularity. NFTs tend to appreciate over time since they are unique. They therefore present an alluring

choice for those searching for non-traditional investment options.

Easy Access

Because NFTs are available to anyone, they are growing in popularity. A digital wallet and an internet connection are all needed to buy an NFT. Because of this, anyone from anywhere in the globe can use NFTs, regardless of their financial situation or geographic location.

Increasing Demand

The fact that demand for digital collectibles has been rising quickly in recent years is another factor contributing to NFTs' popularity. The popularity of online marketplaces and e-commerce has increased demand for digital asset ownership and trading.

The acceptance of Blockchain Technology

Lastly, the growing acceptance of blockchain technology is a contributing factor to the popularity of NFTs. The use of NFTs is anticipated to increase along with the broader adoption of blockchain technology. This is so because NFTs, as an advantageous alternative to more conventional forms of digital ownership, are a logical application of blockchain technology.

Potential NFT Drawbacks

The popularity of non-fungible tokens (NFTs) has increased recently, however, there may be disadvantages to take into account, just like with any new technology. The following are six possible drawbacks of NFTs:

- ❖ **Limited Liquidity:** Because NFTs are singular, one-of-a-kind assets, their liquidity may be restricted. This implies that selling or trading NFTs could be challenging, particularly if there isn't much of a market for a specific NFT. Due to this lack of liquidity, it could be challenging for consumers to invest in NFTs and make money from them.
- ❖ **Technical Difficulty:** Many people find it challenging to comprehend and utilize blockchain technology, which powers NFTs. Because of their technical complexity, NFTs may not be adopted as widely and may be more challenging for users to comprehend and apply.
- ❖ **Absence of Regulation:** NFTs are currently subject to little regulation, which may allow for possible abuses and scams. Due to the lack of regulation, individuals who invest in NFTs without having a

thorough understanding of the market or technology run the danger of suffering financial losses.

❖ **High Entry Cost:** Individuals and businesses must have access to costly technology, such as specialist software and top-tier graphics cards, to compete in the NFT market. This high barrier to entry may restrict the number of individuals and businesses that can enter the NFT sector.

❖ **Limited Adoption:** Although NFTs are gaining popularity, a large adoption is still necessary, as the technology is still in its infancy. This suggests that there might only be a small number of applications and a small amount of demand for NFTs, which could restrict their overall development and success.

❖ **Environmental Concerns:** The blockchain technology that powers NFTs uses a lot of energy to operate and maintain. Concerns over NFTs' carbon footprint and potential environmental effects have been brought up by their energy usage.

NFTs' Future and Its Effect on Society

In the fields of technology and art, there is a lot of discussion about the future of NFTs and how they will affect society. Their capacity to symbolize ownership and authenticity of digital assets, such as art, and collectibles, has made them more well-known in recent years.

The following topics address NFTs' future and the effects they will have on society.

Influence on Customary Ownership Techniques

NFTs have the power to upend established practices in asset transfer and ownership. NFTs, for instance, can be used to transfer ownership without the need for middlemen like banks or attorneys and to represent ownership of digital goods like music and films.

This can result in lower expenses and more efficiency.

The Future of Collecting

NFTs have the power to completely change how we exchange and gather both digital and physical goods. Because of its distinctiveness, each NFT is guaranteed to be one of a kind, and they offer a safe and transparent method of transferring ownership. As a result, NFTs are probably going to become more valuable and in demand in the future.

NFTs' Extension into New Industries

NFTs have already demonstrated promise in several sectors, including entertainment and gaming. NFTs will probably find new applications in a variety of different industries, including finance and real estate, as technology develops. Businesses and people will have more options to employ NFTs to produce and exchange digital assets as a result of this increase.

Enhanced Uptake and Acceptance

The popularity of NFTs is rising as more individuals become aware of their advantages. We therefore anticipate an increase in their use across several sectors, including entertainment, gaming, and the arts. New NFT platforms and marketplaces are probably going to be developed as a result of this growing popularity.

Increased Recognition in the Art World

The acceptance of NFTs in the art world is growing, and this industry will continue to use them more and more. This is so that buyers can demonstrate their ownership and artists can sell and validate their creations in a new way thanks to NFTs. The value of NFTs and the art market will probably increase as a result.

Conclusion

The potential for Non-Fungible Tokens (NFTs) to transform ownership and commerce in the physical world is immense. NFTs have the power to alter the way we think about purchasing and selling products and services by establishing a new market for resale as well as demonstrating ownership and authenticity. We anticipate seeing an increasing number of NFTs deployed in novel and creative ways as the infrastructure and technology supporting them develop further.

www.ingramcontent.com/pod-product-compliance
Lightning Source LLC
Chambersburg PA
CBHW070954220526
45471CB00007B/3024